I0426155

June 2012

NATIONAL SECURITY

DOD Should Reevaluate Requirements for the Selective Service System

GAO
Accountability * Integrity * Reliability

GAO-12-623

NATIONAL SECURITY

DOD Should Reevaluate Requirements for the Selective Service System

Highlights

Highlights of GAO-12-623, a report to congressional committees

Why GAO Did This Study

The Selective Service System is an independent agency in the executive branch. Its responsibilities include maintaining a database that will enable it to provide manpower to DOD in a national emergency, managing a program for conscientious objectors to satisfy their obligations through a program of civilian service, and ensuring the capability to register and induct medical personnel if directed to do so. Section 597 of the National Defense Authorization Act for Fiscal Year 2012 (Pub. L. No. 112-81) requires that GAO assess the military necessity of the Selective Service System and examine alternatives to its current structure. Specifically, GAO (1) determined the extent to which DOD has evaluated the necessity of the Selective Service System to meeting DOD's future manpower requirements beyond the all-volunteer force and (2) reviewed the fiscal and national security considerations of various alternatives to the Selective Service System. GAO reviewed legislation, analyzed relevant documents, verified cost data provided by the Selective Service System, and interviewed DOD, Office of Management and Budget, and Selective Service System officials.

What GAO Recommends

GAO recommends that DOD (1) evaluate its requirements for the Selective Service System in light of recent strategic guidance and (2) establish a process of periodically reevaluating these requirements. In written comments on a draft of this report, DOD agreed with the recommendations.

View GAO-12-623. For more information, contact Brenda S. Farrell at (202) 512-3604 or farrel b@gao.gov.

What GAO Found

The Department of Defense (DOD) has not recently evaluated the necessity of the Selective Service System to meeting DOD's future manpower requirements for carrying out the defense strategy or reexamined time frames for inducting personnel in the event of a draft. DOD officials told GAO that the Selective Service System provides a low-cost insurance policy in case a draft is ever necessary. The Selective Service System maintains a structure that would help ensure the equity and credibility of a draft. For example, the Selective Service System manages the registration of males aged 18 through 25 and maintains no-cost agreements with organizations that would offer alternative service to conscientious objectors. The Selective Service System also has unpaid volunteers who could be activated as soon as a draft is enacted to review claims for deferment. However, DOD has not used the draft since 1973, and because of its reliance and emphasis on the all-volunteer force, DOD has not reevaluated requirements for the Selective Service System since 1994, although significant changes to the national security environment have occurred since that time. Periodically reevaluating an agency's requirements is critical to helping ensure that resources are appropriately matched to requirements that represent today's environment. Selective Service System officials expressed concern that, as currently resourced, they cannot meet DOD's requirements to deliver inductees without jeopardizing the fairness and equity of the draft. However, the lack of an updated requirement from DOD presents challenges to policymakers for determining whether the Selective Service System is properly resourced or necessary.

Restructuring or disestablishing the Selective Service System would require consideration of various fiscal and national security implications. GAO reviewed data on costs and savings associated with maintaining the Selective Service System's current operations, operating in a deep standby mode with active registration, and disestablishing the Selective Service System altogether.

Estimated Costs and Savings of Current Operations and Alternatives

Dollars in millions

	Maintaining current operations	Deep standby with registration	Disestablishment
Estimated first-year savings	$0	$4.8	$17.9
Estimated recurring savings	$0	$6.6	$24.4
Estimated budget after implementation	$24.4	$17.8	$0

Source: Selective Service System.

Note: Numbers may not add up due to rounding.

If Congress disestablishes the Selective Service System it would need to amend the Military Selective Service Act and potentially other laws involving the Selective Service System. There are also limitations that would need to be considered if Selective Service System functions were transferred to another agency. Selective Service System officials said that while other databases could be used for a registration database, these databases might not lead to a fair and equitable draft because they would not be as complete and would therefore put some portions of the population at a higher risk of being drafted than others.

_____ United States Government Accountability Office

Contents

United States Government Accountability Office
Washington, DC 20548

June 7, 2012

Congressional Committees

Under the Military Selective Service Act,[1] the Selective Service System is an independent agency within the executive branch of the federal government.[2] Its responsibilities include maintaining a registration database that will enable it to provide untrained manpower to the Department of Defense (DOD) in the event of a national emergency, managing a program for conscientious objectors to satisfy their obligations through a program of alternative civilian service, and ensuring the capability to register and induct medical personnel if directed to do so.

We conducted this review in response to the mandate in section 597 of the National Defense Authorization Act for Fiscal Year 2012,[3] which requires us to assess the military necessity of the Selective Service System and examine various alternatives to its current structure. Specifically, we (1) determined the extent to which DOD has evaluated the necessity of the Selective Service System to meeting the department's future manpower requirements in excess of the all-volunteer force and (2) reviewed the fiscal and national security considerations of various alternatives to the Selective Service System, including disestablishing the agency, reducing its current capacity, or having its functions performed or database maintained by another organization. Our review did not assess whether or not the Selective Service System should be restructured or disestablished, as this is ultimately a policy decision for Congress.

For our first objective, to determine the extent to which DOD has evaluated the necessity of the Selective Service System to meeting DOD's future manpower requirements in excess of the all-volunteer force, we analyzed documents and guidance on DOD's manpower requirements for the Selective Service System and interviewed DOD and Selective Service System officials on the role and necessity of the Selective Service

---

[1] 50 U.S.C. App. §§ 451—473.

[2] 50 U.S.C. App. § 460(a).

[3] Pub. L. No. 112-81 (2011).

System to meeting DOD's requirements. We also determined whether and how often DOD evaluates its requirements for the Selective Service System. For our second objective, to review the fiscal and national security considerations of various alternatives to the Selective Service System, we requested that officials from the Selective Service System identify the estimated costs, savings, and national security implications of disestablishing the Selective Service System or placing it in a deep standby mode.[4] While we relied on data provided by Selective Service System officials, we examined their assumptions and verified their methodology in calculating the costs of termination and potential savings. We determined that these data were sufficiently reliable for our purpose of providing an estimate of the costs of alternatives to the Selective Service System's current structure. We interviewed DOD and Selective Service System officials to determine whether there are comparable databases or other agencies, including DOD, that could perform the Selective Service System's functions. We also asked them to identify any factors and limitations that might affect the costs of another agency or database replacing the functions of the Selective Service System.

We conducted this performance audit from February to June 2012 in accordance with generally accepted government auditing standards. Those standards require that we plan and perform the audit to obtain sufficient, appropriate evidence to provide a reasonable basis for our findings and conclusions based on our audit objectives. We believe that the evidence obtained provides a reasonable basis for our findings and conclusions based on our audit objectives. Further information on our scope, methodology, and data reliability assessment can be found in appendix I.

Background

The Military Selective Service Act requires virtually all male U.S. citizens worldwide and all other males residing in the United States ages 18 through 25 to register with the Selective Service System within 30 days of turning 18 years of age under procedures established by a presidential proclamation and other rules and regulations. The Selective Service System currently budgets for 130 full-time civilian positions and 175 part-

---

[4]Section 597 of the National Defense Authorization Act for Fiscal Year 2012 defined deep standby mode as the Selective Service System retaining only personnel sufficient to conduct necessary functions, to include maintaining the registration database.

time Reserve Force Officers[5] in its national headquarters in Arlington, Virginia; its Data Management Center, in Chicago, Illinois; and its three regional headquarters, located in Chicago, Illinois; Smyrna, Georgia; and Denver, Colorado. In 2011, the Selective Service System's Data Management Center added 2.2 million records to its database and sent a series of letters to males reminding them of their obligation to register. According to Selective Service System officials, in calendar year 2010, their database contained approximately 16.4 million names, and the estimated registration compliance rate was 92 percent. The Selective Service System also carries out other peacetime activities such as conducting public registration awareness and outreach, responding to public inquiries about registration requirements, and providing training and support to volunteer local board members, state directors, and Reserve Force Officers.

The Military Selective Service Act does not currently authorize use of a draft for the induction of persons into the armed forces. Congress and the President would be required to enact a law authorizing a draft, were they to deem it necessary to supplement the existing force with additional military manpower. In the event of a draft, the Selective Service System would be tasked with conducting a lottery and sending induction notices to selected males to supply the personnel requested by the Secretary of Defense. A network of over 11,000 local, district, and national board volunteers, who are now managed by the Selective Service System, would be activated to review and process claims for exemption, deferment, or postponement of service. Selected males would be directed to report to Military Entrance Processing Stations, managed by DOD, to determine whether they are qualified for military service, and then sent to military training centers. In addition to drafting inductees, the Selective Service System would be responsible for providing options and managing the program for alternative civilian service to conscientious objectors and would also be required to induct health care specialists if necessary.

---

[5]Reserve Force Officers are maintained at a maximum number of 175, which includes 150 funded by the Selective Service System and 25 on loan from the military services.

DOD Has Not Evaluated the Necessity of the Selective Service System Since 1994

The Selective Service System's time frames for mobilizing inductees are based on DOD's recommendations developed in accordance with its manpower requirements as defined in 1994; therefore, the appropriateness of these time frames to helping DOD meet its current manpower needs in excess of the current all-volunteer force is unclear. Even though DOD has not used the draft since 1973, DOD officials told us that the Selective Service System provides a low-cost insurance policy in case a draft is ever necessary and a structure and organization that would help ensure the equity and credibility of a draft should one be authorized and implemented. The Selective Service System also offers capabilities that are hard to quantify in terms of dollars, including its structure of unpaid volunteers who could be activated as soon as a draft is implemented and its no-cost agreements with civilian organizations that have agreed to supply jobs to conscientious objectors. Selective Service System officials expressed concern that, as currently resourced, they cannot meet DOD's requirements to deliver inductees without jeopardizing the fairness and equity of the draft. However, that requirement was based on the national security environment that existed in 1994. The lack of an updated requirement from DOD presents challenges to policymakers for determining whether the Selective Service System is properly resourced or necessary.

The Selective Service System's Current Manpower Requirements Are Based on a 1994 DOD Evaluation

DOD developed its manpower requirements for the Selective Service System in 1994 and has not reexamined these requirements in the context of recent military operations and changes in the security environment and national security strategy. In a 1994 memorandum[6] to the Director of the Selective Service System, the Assistant Secretary of Defense for Force Management stated that DOD expected that its active and reserve forces would be sufficient for most conceivable scenarios involving two Major Regional Conflicts, citing two then-current documents, the 1993 *Report on the Bottom-Up Review* and the 1994 *A National Security Strategy of Engagement and Enlargement*. Because of this expectation, DOD recommended extending the time it would require the Selective Service System to provide the first inductees from 13 days to

---

[6]Assistant Secretary of Defense for Force Management, Memorandum for Director of Selective Service System, "Updated Manpower Requirements" (Nov. 16, 1994). Other, more general guidance is provided in DOD Instruction 1100.19, *Wartime Manpower Mobilization Planning Policies and Procedures* (Feb. 20, 1986) and DOD 1100.19-H, *Wartime Manpower Mobilization Planning Guidance* (Mar. 1990).

193 days after mobilization (13 days plus 6 months) and to provide 100,000 inductees from 30 days to 210 days after mobilization (30 days plus 6 months). The Selective Service System considers this requirement to be its most recent and official requirement from DOD. The memorandum also stated that DOD's position was that an all-male draft remained valid and legal and that medical personnel continued to be the only skilled group that would be required in conceivable contingency scenarios. Specifically, the document states that DOD's Health Care Personnel Delivery System calls for the rapid postmobilization registration of up to 3.5 million health care personnel in more than 60 specialties. DOD also stated in its memorandum that the time for the Selective Service System to conduct a mass registration of medical personnel could be extended by 6 months, from 13 days to 193 days, with induction orders to follow 3 weeks later.

DOD relies on its national defense strategy and the Quadrennial Defense Review to identify its priority mission areas and determine its overall force structure needs.[7] The national defense strategy provides the foundation and strategic framework for the department's Quadrennial Defense Review, which is performed every 4 years. During this review, DOD is required to define a national defense strategy and the force structure and other elements necessary to successfully execute the range of missions identified in that national defense strategy. Changes in the security environment require the department and the services to reassess their force structure requirements, including how many and what types of units are necessary to carry out the national defense strategy. For example, as DOD stated in its January 2012 strategic guidance, even when U.S. forces are committed to a large-scale operation in one region, they will need to be capable of denying the objectives of—or imposing unacceptable costs on—an opportunistic aggressor in a second region. Specifically, the United States will need to be prepared for an increasingly complex set of challenges in South Asia, the Middle East, and the Asia-Pacific region.[8]

In prior work, we have emphasized the importance of agencies taking actions to ensure that their missions are current and that their

---

[7]Force structure represents the numbers, size, and composition of the units that comprise U.S. forces.

[8]*Sustaining U.S. Global Leadership: Priorities for 21st Century Defense* (January 2012).

organizations are structured to meet those missions. We have also reported that many agencies find themselves encumbered with structures and processes rooted in the past and designed to meet the demands of earlier times.[9] Further, we have stated that high-performing organizations stay alert to emerging mission demands and remain open to reevaluating their human capital practices to meet emerging agency needs.[10] Changes in the security environment and defense strategy represent junctures at which DOD can systematically reevaluate service personnel levels to determine whether they are consistent with strategic objectives.

While DOD officials stated that the 1994 manpower requirement may still be valid, without an updated assessment of requirements for the Selective Service System, policymakers cannot be certain whether the resources to support the Selective Service System are necessary to meet DOD's manpower needs, whether the Selective Service System is prepared to supply the skills most critical to DOD in the 21st century, or whether the Selective Service System is necessary at all. In a letter to GAO dated April 16, 2012, the Deputy Assistant Secretary for Military Personnel Policy stated that determining the military necessity for the Selective Service System and its registration of young men is a complex issue that requires significant examination not possible during the period of GAO's review.[11] However, DOD does recognize that such an examination is prudent. The Deputy Assistant Secretary noted that, while the military necessity of the Selective Service System in the 21st century has yet to be determined, the department recognizes that there are benefits to the continuation of the Selective Service System.

---

[9]GAO, *Executive Guide: Effectively Implementing the Government Performance and Results Act*, GAO/GGD-96-118 (Washington, D.C.: June 1996).

[10]GAO, *A Model of Strategic Human Capital Management*, GAO-02-373SP (Washington, D.C.: Mar. 15, 2002).

[11]Section 597 of the National Defense Authorization Act for Fiscal Year 2012, dated December 2011, required GAO to provide a report containing the results of our study to the Committees on Armed Services of the Senate and House of Representatives no later than May 1, 2012. To satisfy this mandate, we provided a draft of this report to the Committees on that date.

Selective Service System Said It Is Not Resourced to Meet DOD's Requirements but Provides a Structure That Could Be Used for a Fair and Equitable Draft

According to official spokespersons for the Selective Service System, the agency is not currently resourced to meet DOD's requirement for it to deliver the first inductees in 193 days and 100,000 inductees in 210 days, without jeopardizing the fairness and equity of the draft. However, DOD officials believe that the Selective Service System provides a low-cost insurance policy in case a draft is ever necessary. The Selective Service System also provides benefits that would help to ensure a draft was fair and equitable. Specifically, Selective Service System officials stated that since fiscal year 1997, the agency has undergone various cuts and attained efficiencies in an attempt to meet DOD's manpower requirements. The Selective Service System officials said that due to reductions in the number of personnel available to set up area offices across the country, it now estimates it could not deliver the first inductees until 285 days after mobilization. In fiscal year 1997, the Selective Service System's budget was $22.9 million (in then-year dollars), or $31.5 million in fiscal year 2013 dollars. Since then, the agency's annual budget has declined steadily in constant dollars, and its requested budget for fiscal year 2013 was $24.4 million.[12]

According to the Selective Service System's fiscal year 2011 Annual Report, maintaining acceptable registration compliance rates of at least 90 percent is key to the agency's ability to conduct a fair and equitable draft, should it be necessary. Maintaining a high compliance rate, Selective Service System officials believe, helps to ensure that the highest possible number of eligible men are targeted equally. Within its available budget, the Selective Service System is able to maintain registration compliance rates of 69 percent for 18-year-old males, 89 percent for 19-year-old males, and 96 percent for 20- through 25-year-old males.[13] The Selective Service System estimates that over the past few years, a larger portion of the registration process has become automated because many state drivers' license programs now require registration with the Selective Service System as a prerequisite, and the Selective Service System offers internet and telephone registration options. However, Selective Service System's data-entry staff also input over

---

[12]Constant dollars measure the value of purchased goods and services at price levels that are the same as the reference year. Constant dollars do not contain any adjustments for inflationary changes that have occurred or are forecast to occur outside the reference year.

[13]Once a man reaches his 26th birthday, his name is dropped from the Selective Service System's list of possible draftees.

712,000 transactions each year, including manual registrations, registrant file updates, compliance additions and updates, post office returns, and miscellaneous forms. The Data Management Center also serves as the agency's national call center, which the public contacts to verify registrations that are needed to be eligible for benefits and programs linked to this registration, such as student loans and government jobs. In addition, the Selective Service System undertakes general national outreach and public awareness initiatives to publicize the requirement for males to register. These efforts have included convention exhibits, public service announcements, high school publicity kits, focus group studies, and outreach meetings. The Selective Service System also conducts outreach visits to areas of low registration compliance.

In addition to registration, the Selective Service System structure helps to ensure that a draft would be fair and equitable. For example, it maintains a structure that could be activated as soon as a draft is implemented to conduct nationwide local review boards to determine draftees' eligibility for deferments. The Selective Service System's three regional offices are responsible for maintaining this board structure and making sure that personnel are trained to perform their assigned tasks. Each state and territory has a part-time state director who is compensated for an average of up to 12 duty days per year. In 2011, the Selective Service System also relied on 175 Reserve Force Officers from all branches of the military services. These part-time officers perform peacetime and preparedness tasks, such as training civilian board members, and function as field contacts for state and local agencies and the public. The largest component of the Selective Service System's workforce is approximately 11,000 uncompensated men and women. According to Selective Service System officials, these men and women are selected to be representatives of the geographic area in which they reside and are trained to serve as volunteer local, district, and national appeal board members. If a draft were to occur, these trained volunteers would decide the classification status of men seeking exceptions or deferments based on conscientious objection, hardship to dependents, their status as ministers or ministerial students, or any other reason. Selective Service System officials believe that having local board members representative of the geographic areas in which they reside helps to ensure that these board members would make fair and equitable decisions.

If a draft occurred, the Selective Service System is also required to manage a 2-year program of alternative civilian service for conscientious objectors. The Selective Service System maintains no-cost agreements with civilian organizations that, in the event of a draft, have agreed to supply jobs to conscientious objectors who oppose any form of military service, even in a noncombat capacity. To be prepared to implement an alternative service program for registrants classified as conscientious objectors, the Selective Service System conducts outreach to various civilian employers, such as the Methuselah Foundation and the Mennonite Mission Network, to arrange memoranda of agreement for these organizations to be prepared to offer alternative service to up to 30,000 conscientious objectors should a draft be necessary.

Restructuring or Disestablishing the Selective Service System Requires Consideration of Fiscal and National Security Implications

Restructuring or disestablishing the Selective Service System would require consideration of various fiscal and national security implications, some of which may be difficult to quantify. We reviewed estimated costs and savings for two alternatives to the current structure of the Selective Service System: (1) placing it in a deep standby mode where active registration is maintained and (2) disestablishing the agency. In addition to the potential costs and savings of these alternatives, other factors, with both tangible and intangible costs and benefits, may need to be considered if either alternative were pursued. We identified factors that may affect costs and various considerations and limitations that may affect whether another agency or database could perform the functions of the Selective Service System while maintaining the capability to perform a fair and equitable draft.

Options for Disestablishing or Restructuring the Selective Service System Differ in Cost, Savings, and Personnel Requirements

Officials from the Selective Service System provided details on the personnel and resources required for each of the alternatives we reviewed, as well as their estimated cost savings (see table 1). The Selective Service System estimates were based on the assumption that either alternative would be fully implemented in fiscal year 2013, and officials based their estimates on their fiscal year 2013 requested budget. Most of the estimated cost savings result from reductions in the numbers of civilian and Reserve Force Officer personnel for the two alternatives we examined.

Table 1: Estimated Costs and Savings of Current Operations and Alternatives to the Selective Service System

Dollars in millions

	Maintaining current operations	Deep standby with registration	Disestablishment
Personnel required			
Civilian (full-time, paid)	130	93	0
Reserve Force Officers (part-time, paid)	150	0	0
Reserve Force Officers (part-time, unpaid)	25	0	0
State directors (part-time, paid)	56	0	0
Civilian board members (unpaid)	11,000	0	0
Estimated first-year savings after termination costs are subtracted	$0	$4.8	$17.9
Estimated recurring annual savings	$0	$6.6	$24.4
Estimated budget after implementation	$24.4	$17.8	$0

Source: Selective Service System

Notes: Numbers may not add up due to rounding.

The figures in this table are based on Selective Service System's estimates of the number of personnel required and potential costs and savings for the agency to be put in a deep standby mode or disestablished. These estimates are based on the assumption that a decision to restructure or disestablish the Selective Service System would be made in the first quarter of the fiscal year and completed by the end of the fiscal year. The budgets identified in the table correspond with the estimated budgets after the scenario is implemented.

The Selective Service System's current budget authorizes 130 civilian full-time equivalent positions. Three of those authorized positions represent the funds necessary to pay the part-time salaries of the 56 state directors.

The potential savings identified in both the deep standby with registration and disestablishment scenarios assume approximately $2.6 million in savings associated with dismissing the part-time paid Reserve Force Officers. These savings may not be realized if these positions are absorbed by the Department of Defense.

As shown in table 1, if the Selective Service System were placed in a deep standby mode and maintained its registration program and database, Selective Service System officials estimated that the first-year cost savings would be approximately $4.8 million, with subsequent annual savings of approximately $6.6 million. Selective Service System officials estimated that costs for closing the regional offices, severance pay, and other termination costs would be $1.8 million. The Selective Service System estimates it would require a budget of $17.8 million and 93 full-time civilian personnel at the national headquarters and Data Management Center to continue inputting and processing registrations, maintain registration awareness and compliance, and facilitate plans to reconstitute the agency if needed. The estimates assume that the Selective Service System would reduce its civilian workforce by 37 positions, would no longer employ Reserve Force Officers or state directors, and would reduce its physical infrastructure costs by closing its three regional offices.

According to Selective Service System officials, disestablishing the agency would produce first-year cost savings of approximately $17.9 million and subsequent annual savings of $24.4 million. This scenario assumes that all full-time civilians, Reserve Force Officers, and state directors would be terminated or dismissed, and the agency headquarters, three regional headquarters, and data management center would be closed. Selective Service System officials estimated that costs for closing the agency and terminating employees and contracts would total approximately $6.5 million in the first year. In both of the alternatives presented in table 1, the 11,000 civilian volunteer board members would be dismissed, eliminating the volunteer board infrastructure currently in place to review claims for deferring or postponing military service.

Selective Service System officials also identified the estimated time and potential resources required to reestablish the agency to its current operations should either of these options be pursued.[14] Selective Service System officials estimated that if the agency were in a deep standby mode or disestablished, it would cost approximately $6.6 and $28 million,[15] respectively, to restore the agency to its current operating capacity. Officials estimated that if the agency were put in a deep standby mode with registration, it would take approximately 18 months to rehire and train essential civilian and Reserve Force Officer personnel,

---

[14]The Selective Service System's estimates for the time required to reconstitute the agency to the current status quo are based on its experiences transitioning from deep standby to full operations in 1980.

[15]Selective Service System officials estimated that if the agency were disestablished, they would require their fiscal year 2013 estimated budget of $24.4 million plus an additional $3.6 million to build an information technology system for the registration database.

reestablish regional offices, and appoint state directors and civilian volunteer board members. If the agency were disestablished, officials estimated it would take an additional 6 months—or a total of approximately 2 years—to perform mass registrations, reconstitute the Data Management Center and regional offices, build the necessary information technology infrastructure, and rehire and train personnel.

Selective Service System officials also provided estimates for the time and resources required to perform a draft from its current operations if the agency were in deep standby or disestablished. According to Selective Service System officials, they have no previous experience transitioning from disestablishment or a standby mode to draft operations. While their estimates are loosely based on the agency's mobilization plans, officials noted that their plans have not recently been updated and do not reflect their current staffing or budget. To perform a draft from its current operating status, Selective Service System officials said that they would require approximately $465 million to hire the full-time civilian personnel necessary to populate the field structure by staffing area and alternative service offices and district and local boards. If either deep standby or disestablishment were pursued and a draft became necessary, Selective Service System officials said they would need funds in addition to the $465 million it would currently require to perform a draft. Selective Service System officials estimated that if the agency were in a standby mode or disestablished, they would require approximately 830 days and 920 days, respectively, to provide DOD with inductees.

In addition to the potential costs and savings for each option, officials from the Selective Service System and DOD identified other factors that would need to be considered if the agency were disestablished or placed in a deep standby mode. Officials reaffirmed several benefits that they stated had been previously identified in a 1994 National Security Council recommendation to maintain the Selective Service System and the registration program. For example, DOD and Selective Service System officials said that the presence of a registration system and the Selective Service System demonstrates a feeling of resolve on the part of the United States to potential adversaries. Officials also stated that, as fewer citizens have direct contact with military service, registering with the Selective Service System may be the only link some young men will have to military service and the all-volunteer force. Selective Service System officials noted that the Selective Service System and registration requirement provide a hedge against unforeseen threats. Officials from DOD also cited some secondary recruiting benefits they receive from the Selective Service System. DOD relies on the Selective Service System to mail out recruiting pamphlets in conjunction with the registration materials the agency routinely sends to new registrants. DOD officials told us that using the Selective Service System to mail these materials costs approximately $370,000 a year, which is significantly less than the department would spend on postage to mail the recruiting materials separately and which results in approximately 60,000 recruiting leads a year. In addition, DOD officials said that DOD relies heavily on the Selective Service System's database to help populate its recruiting and marketing database at no cost to the department.

Other costs and considerations may need to be evaluated as well. A number of federal and state programs require registration as a prerequisite, such as state drivers' licenses and identification cards, federal student aid programs, U.S. citizenship, federally sponsored job training, and government employment. Selective Service System officials said there could be costs to remove language from forms and program materials stating that registering with the Selective Service System is a prerequisite to qualifying for these programs. Furthermore, Selective Service System officials said that agreements with civilian agencies to provide alternative civilian service for conscientious objectors would be terminated if registration were discontinued or the agency were disestablished, and reinstituting these agreements in the event of a draft would take time. Terminating the Selective Service System would also require amending the Military Selective Service Act and potentially other laws involving the Selective Service System.

Transferring Selective Service System's Functions to Another Agency Could Affect the Independence and Fairness of a Draft and May Not Be Cost-Efficient

Selective Service System and DOD officials identified factors that should be considered if the functions of the Selective Service System were to be performed by another federal or state agency or with another database. We were unable to identify specific costs associated with these options because, according to officials from DOD and the Selective Service System, there is no database that is comparable to or as complete as the Selective Service System's database. However, officials did identify several factors and limitations that could affect the costs and feasibility of having the Selective Service System's functions performed by another entity.

Officials from the Selective Service System identified several databases and agencies that currently help populate their registration database. For example, Selective Service System officials said they have agreements with the Social Security Administration and the American Association of Motor Vehicles to supply names of 18- through 25-year-olds[16] who have registered social security numbers or who apply for drivers' licenses, at a cost of $14,200 and $42,177 a year, respectively. Selective Service System officials also said they rely on the U.S. Census Bureau to provide a breakdown of the total number of men aged 18 through 25 by state and county, which the Selective Service System uses to determine its overall registration compliance rate. Selective Service System officials agreed that other agencies' databases, like those of the Social Security Administration and the American Association of Motor Vehicles, could be used or combined to populate a registration database but noted that a draft using these systems might not be fair and equitable because these databases would target certain portions of the pool of possible inductees but not others. For example, if a draft were performed using only names in the Social Security Administration's database, immigrant men residing in the United States who do not have social security numbers would not have the same likelihood of being drafted as male U.S. citizens would. Selective Service System officials also stated that there could be costs associated with combining other databases to achieve the compliance rate of the Selective Service System's database. The Selective Service System database represents 92 percent of the eligible population, and Selective Service System officials said they rely on a number of sources to maintain a high registration compliance rate and have established a process that gives everyone an equal chance of being selected. The Selective Service System therefore believes it can perform a fair and equitable draft of the population and said that other databases, unless similarly combined, could not replicate the completeness of the Selective Service System database.

DOD and Selective Service System officials also expressed concern with having another federal agency perform the Selective Service System's functions. Selective Service System officials said that any transfer of their responsibilities to DOD or another federal agency would raise independence concerns with respect to ensuring that a draft would be fair

---

[16]Though 18- through 25-year-olds are required to register, once a man reaches his 26th birthday, his name is dropped from the Selective Service System's list of possible draftees.

and equitable.[17] For example, according to Selective Service System officials, the independence of the agency helps to ensure that conscientious objector and pacifist communities will comply with registration requirements because the public trusts that the registration and induction process is performed fairly. DOD officials said that a significant evaluation would need to be performed to determine the costs and feasibility of the department taking on the Selective Service System's tasks and that they are unable to identify the potential costs for the department to assume the responsibilities of the Selective Service System. DOD officials were able to provide the approximate costs to maintain the department's recruiting and marketing database, but they emphasized that this database would be inappropriate to use as a replacement for the Selective Service System's database because the Joint Advertising Market Research and Studies office relies on third-party data to populate its database, which is used strictly for the purpose of performing recruiting and market research. Officials from DOD's Joint Advertising Market Research and Studies office indicated that their office currently spends approximately $2.8 million a year to operate and maintain their database of recruiting and marketing names and that it would cost an additional $3 million to replace the names it receives from the Selective Service System free of charge, more than doubling DOD's operating costs for this database. In addition, DOD and Selective Service System officials stated that they are uncertain whether any savings would be realized by transferring the Selective Service System's function to DOD or any other federal agency. Officials said the same number of personnel and resources would likely be required, and according to Selective Service System officials, there could be additional costs involved in having another agency learn how to recreate the components of the Selective Service System.

Conclusions

While the Selective Service System states that it is not resourced to provide first inductees within 193 days of mobilization and 100,000 inductees within 210 days, DOD has not reevaluated this requirement since 1994. Since that time, the security environment and the national security strategy have changed significantly. Without an updated assessment by DOD of its specific requirements for the Selective Service

---

[17]In addition, Congress declared in the Military Selective Service Act that, as a matter of policy, "the Selective Service System should remain administratively independent of any other agency, including the Department of Defense." 50 U.S.C. App. § 451(f).

System, it is unclear whether DOD would need 100,000 inductees in 210 days or even whether draftees would play any role in a military mobilization. Further, while DOD officials believe that the Selective Service System provides a low-cost insurance policy and benefits DOD in other ways—some that are hard to quantify—determining the value of these benefits is ultimately a policy decision for Congress, as is the determination of the cost and benefit trade-offs of the various alternatives to reducing the agency or transferring its functions. A reevaluation of the department's manpower needs for the Selective Service System in light of current national security plans would better position Congress to make an informed decision about the necessity of the Selective Service System or any other alternatives that might substitute for it.

Recommendations for Executive Action

To help ensure that DOD and Congress have visibility over the necessity of the Selective Service System to meeting DOD's needs, we recommend that the Secretary of Defense direct the Under Secretary of Defense for Personnel and Readiness to take the following two actions:

(1) evaluate DOD's requirements for the Selective Service System in light of recent strategic guidance and report the results of this evaluation to Congress and

(2) establish a process of periodically reevaluating DOD's requirements for the Selective Service System in light of changing threats, operating environments, and strategic guidance.

Agency Comments and Our Evaluation

In commenting on a draft of this report, DOD agreed with our recommendations and noted its plans for implementation. Specifically, DOD concurred with our first recommendation—to evaluate DOD's requirements for the Selective Service System to reflect recent strategic guidance and report the results of its evaluation to Congress. The department stated that the Office of the Under Secretary of Defense for Personnel and Readiness, in coordination with the Joint Staff and the services, will perform an analysis of DOD's manpower requirements for the Selective Service System, with an anticipated completion date of December 1, 2012. DOD also concurred with our second recommendation—to establish a process to periodically reevaluate DOD's requirements for the Selective Service System in light of changing threats, operating environments, and strategic guidance. The department stated that it will establish a process to review the mission and requirements for the Selective Service System during its reevaluation of its current requirements for the Selective Service System. DOD's comments are reprinted in appendix II.

We also provided a draft of this report to the Selective Service System for comment. In its written comments, the Selective Service System noted its support of DOD's views of the Selective Service System. Specifically, it cited the Secretary of Defense's 2011 testimony in support of maintaining registration as a mechanism to ensure the department is prepared for an unexpected event. The Selective Service System's comments are reprinted in appendix III. The Selective Service System also provided technical comments, which we incorporated as appropriate. We also provided the Office of Management and Budget a draft, but we did not receive any comments.

We are sending copies of this report to appropriate congressional committees; the Secretary of Defense; the Under Secretary of Defense for Personnel and Readiness; and the Director of the Selective Service. We will also make copies available to other interested parties upon request. In addition, the report will be available at no charge on the GAO website at http://www.gao.gov. If you have any questions about this report, please contact me at (202) 512-3604 or farrellb@gao.gov. Major contributors to this report are listed in appendix IV.

Brenda S. Farrell
Director, Defense Capabilities and Management

List of Committees

The Honorable Carl Levin
Chairman
The Honorable John McCain
Ranking Member
Committee on Armed Services
United States Senate

The Honorable Howard "Buck" McKeon
Chairman
The Honorable Adam Smith
Ranking Member
Committee on Armed Services
House of Representatives

Appendix I: Scope and Methodology

To determine the extent to which the Department of Defense (DOD) has evaluated the necessity of the Selective Service System to meeting DOD's future manpower requirements in excess of the all-volunteer force, we analyzed documentation and information obtained from interviews with relevant officials from the Office of the Under Secretary of Defense for Personnel and Readiness, Office of Management and Budget, and Selective Service System. To determine DOD's manpower requirements, we reviewed DOD guidance and documents, including guidance on wartime manpower mobilization procedures and mobilization requirements. We also analyzed Selective Service System annual reports and budget justification documents, as well as input provided by the Selective Service System to the Office of Management and Budget. We reviewed relevant legislation establishing the Selective Service System and registration requirements in title 50 of the United States Code. We obtained DOD and Selective Service System officials' perspectives on the role of the Selective Service System, as well as the Selective Service's ability to meet its current need for inductees as defined by DOD's manpower mobilization requirements. To obtain criteria for how frequently agencies should reevaluate their missions, we consulted our body of work on this subject.[1]

To review the fiscal and national security considerations of various alternatives to the Selective Service System, we obtained cost estimates from Selective Service System officials for two scenarios involving reducing or eliminating the Selective Service System: (1) disestablishing the Selective Service System and (2) placing the agency in a standby mode while having it continue to register potential draftees. We interviewed Selective Service System officials to identify their assumptions and sources for calculating the costs to implement these two scenarios. To assess the reliability of their cost estimates, we gathered and analyzed the agency's budget documents to verify their calculations and assumptions and provided updates to the estimates for the Selective Service System to review. To assess the reliability of computer-processed data used to estimate costs, we interviewed Selective Service System

---

[1]GAO, *Executive Guide: Effectively Implementing the Government Performance and Results Act*, GAO/GGD-96-118 (Washington, D.C.: June 1996); *Model of Strategic Human Capital Management*, GAO-02-373SP (Washington, D.C.: Mar. 15, 2002); and *Military Personnel: DOD Needs to Conduct a Data-Driven Analysis of Active Military Personnel Levels Required to Implement the Defense Strategy*, GAO-05-200 (Washington, D.C.: Feb. 1, 2005).

officials and obtained documentation from the Department of the Interior to confirm the data and internal controls used in the system. We determined that the data were sufficiently reliable for the purposes of this audit. We also interviewed DOD and Selective Service System officials to identify and describe federal or state agencies or comparable databases that could replace the Selective Service System's registration database. We obtained DOD and Selective Service System officials' perspectives about the considerations and potential limitations involved in using another agency or database, as well as factors that could affect the cost and feasibility of another agency or database being used to perform the functions of the Selective Service System. We also reviewed GAO's previous reports on the Selective Service System.[2]

We conducted this performance audit from February to June 2012 in accordance with generally accepted government auditing standards. Those standards require that we plan and perform the audit to obtain sufficient, appropriate evidence to provide a reasonable basis for our findings and conclusions based on our audit objectives. We believe that the evidence obtained provides a reasonable basis for our findings and conclusions based on our audit objectives.

---

[2]GAO, *Selective Service: Cost and Implications of Two Alternatives to the Present System,* GAO/NSIAD-97-225 (Washington, D.C.: Sept. 20, 1997); *Gender Issues: Changes Would Be Needed to Expand Selective Service Registration to Women,* GAO/NSIAD-98-199 (Washington, D.C.: June 30, 1998); and *Weaknesses in the Selective Service System's Emergency Registration Plan,* FPCD-79-89 (Washington, D.C.: Aug. 29, 1979).

Appendix II: Comments from the Department of Defense

OFFICE OF THE ASSISTANT SECRETARY OF DEFENSE
4000 DEFENSE PENTAGON
WASHINGTON. D.C. 20301-4000

READINESS AND FORCE
MANAGEMENT

2 8 MAY 2012

Ms. Brenda S. Farrell
Director, Defense Capabilities and Management
U.S. Government Accountability Office
441 G. Street, N.W.
Washington, DC 20548

Dear Ms. Farrell:

This is the Department of Defense's (DoD) response to the Government Accountability Office (GAO) Draft Report, GAO-12-623, "National Security: DOD Should Reevaluate Requirements for the Selective Service System," dated May 1, 2012, (GAO Code 351699). We appreciate the opportunity to comment.

The Department concurs with the report's recommendations that DoD should reevaluate the mission and military requirements for the Selective Service System and establish a process for periodic reevaluations.

The Office of the Under Secretary of Defense for Personnel and Readiness, in concert with the Joint Staff and the Services, will undertake such a reevaluation with a target date for completion no later than December 1, 2012.

The enclosure contains detailed departmental comments on each of the two recommendations identified by the GAO. The Department appreciates the opportunity to comment on the draft report.

Sincerely,

Virginia S. Penrod
Deputy Assistant Secretary
(Military Personnel Policy)

Enclosure:
As stated

GAO Draft Report Dated MAY 1, 2012

GAO-12-623 (GAO CODE 351699)

**"NATIONAL SECURITY: DOD SHOULDF REEVALUATE REQUIREMENTS
FOR THE SELECTIVE SERVICE SYSTEM"**

**DEPARTMENT OF DEFENSE COMMENTS
TO THE GAO RECOMMENDATIONS**

RECOMMENDATION 1: To help ensure that DoD and Congress have visibility over
the necessity of the Selective Service System to meeting DoD's needs, the GAO
recommends that the Secretary of Defense direct the Under Secretary of Defense for
Personnel and Readiness to evaluate DoD requirements for the Selective Service System
in light of recent strategic guidance and report the results of this evaluation to Congress.
(See page 18/GAO Draft Report.)

DoD RESPONSE: Concur

The Department of Defense (DoD) concurs that a revaluation of the mission and
requirements provided to the Selective Service System is appropriate, and will conduct
such an analysis with a target date for completion no later than December 1, 2012.

RECOMMENDATION 2: To help ensure that DoD and Congress have visibility over
the necessity of the Selective Service System to meeting DoD's needs, the GAO
recommends that the Secretary of Defense direct the Under Secretary of Defense for
Personnel and Readiness to establish a process of periodically reevaluating DoD's
requirements for the Selective Service System in light of changing threats, operating
environments, and strategic guidance (See page 18/GAO Draft Report.)

DoD RESPONSE: Concur

During the reevaluation and analysis review discussed in the response to
Recommendation 1, DoD will establish a process for periodic reviews of the mission and
requirements for the Selective Service System.

THE DIRECTOR OF SELECTIVE SERVICE
Arlington, Virginia 22209-2425

May 7, 2012

Brenda S. Farrell
Director, Defense Capabilities
 And Management, U.S. GAO
441 G Street, NW, Room 4440-B
Washington, DC 20548

Dear Ms. Farrell:

I have reviewed your proposed report entitled *National Security: DOD Should Reevaluate Requirements for the Selective Service System* (GAO-12-623) and concur with its scope, methodology, and recommendations.

Further, Selective Service supports the stated views of the DOD, together with Secretary of Defense Leon Panetta's statement before the House Armed Services Committee on October 13, 2011, when asked: "The first one [question] is that we still have a selective service system in place... And so the question is, do we still need it?" The Secretary responded: "On the selective service -- the registration, registration is still required. You're right that there is a system. It's not associated with us. But you know, my view is that we ought to maintain the registration aspect because, particularly as we go through these budget cuts, particularly as we go into the future, if we -- if we face, you know, one of those surprises, if we face one of those crises that suddenly occurs, we've got to have some mechanisms in place in order to be able to respond. And while, you know, right now I have to tell you the volunteer force is the best -- I wouldn't trade it for anything. It really has served its purposes. But I think we always have to be ready for that possible contingency in the future if we suddenly had to face an unexpected event."

It was a pleasure working with the very knowledgeable staff of GAO; each was professional, thorough, and focused on developing the most accurate and documented information for the Congress.

Sincerely,

Lawrence G. Romo

Appendix IV: GAO Contact and Staff Acknowledgments

GAO Contact	Brenda S. Farrell, (202) 512-3604 or farrellB@gao.gov.
Acknowledgments	In addition to the contact above, Margaret Best, Assistant Director, Melissa Blanco, Greg Marchand, Charles Perdue, Meghan Perez, Bev Schladt, and Erik Wilkins-McKee made key contributions to this report.

GAO's Mission	The Government Accountability Office, the audit, evaluation, and investigative arm of Congress, exists to support Congress in meeting its constitutional responsibilities and to help improve the performance and accountability of the federal government for the American people. GAO examines the use of public funds; evaluates federal programs and policies; and provides analyses, recommendations, and other assistance to help Congress make informed oversight, policy, and funding decisions. GAO's commitment to good government is reflected in its core values of accountability, integrity, and reliability.
Obtaining Copies of GAO Reports and Testimony	The fastest and easiest way to obtain copies of GAO documents at no cost is through GAO's website (www.gao.gov). Each weekday afternoon, GAO posts on its website newly released reports, testimony, and correspondence. To have GAO e-mail you a list of newly posted products, go to www.gao.gov and select "E-mail Updates."
Order by Phone	The price of each GAO publication reflects GAO's actual cost of production and distribution and depends on the number of pages in the publication and whether the publication is printed in color or black and white. Pricing and ordering information is posted on GAO's website, http://www.gao.gov/ordering.htm. Place orders by calling (202) 512-6000, toll free (866) 801-7077, or TDD (202) 512-2537. Orders may be paid for using American Express, Discover Card, MasterCard, Visa, check, or money order. Call for additional information.
Connect with GAO	Connect with GAO on Facebook, Flickr, Twitter, and YouTube. Subscribe to our RSS Feeds or E-mail Updates. Listen to our Podcasts. Visit GAO on the web at www.gao.gov.
To Report Fraud, Waste, and Abuse in Federal Programs	Contact: Website: www.gao.gov/fraudnet/fraudnet.htm E-mail: fraudnet@gao.gov Automated answering system: (800) 424-5454 or (202) 512-7470
Congressional Relations	Katherine Siggerud, Managing Director, siggerudk@gao.gov, (202) 512-4400, U.S. Government Accountability Office, 441 G Street NW, Room 7125, Washington, DC 20548
Public Affairs	Chuck Young, Managing Director, youngc1@gao.gov, (202) 512-4800 U.S. Government Accountability Office, 441 G Street NW, Room 7149 Washington, DC 20548